Contents

The Christian Prepper's HANDBOOK

A guide to *Surviving a Significant Life Altering Event*

Don't be scared

Don't panic

Just prepare

Zion Prepper

ISBN: 1467918644
ISBN-13: 9781467918640

¹The LORD is my shepherd; I shall not want.
²He maketh me to lie down in green pastures:
he leadeth me beside the still waters.
³He restoreth my soul: he leadeth me in the paths of
righteousness for his name's sake.
⁴Yea, though I walk through the valley of the shadow
of death, I will fear no evil: for thou art with me;
thy rod and thy staff they comfort me.
⁵Thou preparest a table before me in the presence of
mine enemies: thou anointest my head with oil;
my cup runneth over.
⁶Surely goodness and mercy shall follow me all the
days of my life: and I will dwell in the house of the
LORD forever.

PSALM 23 (KJV)

Introduction

The purpose of this handbook is to provide information to the individual, family, church, or group that wants to learn about Christian Prepping or becoming a Christian Prepper. Throughout the book,

I provide descriptions and understanding based on the Christian Preppers mindset. In addition, I offer examples of Christian Prepping and instructions on how to prep that are directly beneficial for the reader. So what is a Christian Prepper? **In its simplest form, Christian Preppers are individuals, families, or groups that are prepared BEFORE a significant event occurs.** A formal definition of a Prepper is the following:

"Prepper (noun): An individual or group that prepares or makes preparations in advance of, or prior to, any <u>change in normal circumstances or lifestyle</u> without significant reliance on other persons (i.e., being self-reliant), or without substantial assistance from outside resources (govt., etc.) in order to minimize the effects of that change on their current lifestyle"(Riverwalker, 2009). According to *InvestmentWatch* there are approximately four million Preppers in the United States, and the number is growing (*InvestmentWatch*, 2011).

As a Christian I know that Prepping has had a profound impact on my family, church, and community. For example, there have been friends who lost their jobs and because of my preparations (preps) I was ready to assist. I was prepared to provide food, batteries, medicine, and fuel to name a few. Had I not been properly prepared I would not have been in the position to support my fellow brother and sisters during their time of crisis. Preppers call these significant events a SLAE (Significant Life Altering Event) scenario. In some instances Preppers believe that these events could potentially lead to a WROL (World without Rule or Law). Prepping sounds simple, but as you will soon realize, Preppers take preparedness to a whole new level. Preppers come in all shapes and sizes. They come from different economic classes, backgrounds, professions, and they have a vast array of experiences. The common bond amongst all Preppers is that they've prepared for the unknown as much as their experience and finances allow. Though not all Preppers prepare the same way, you can count on the fact that they will be ready, and maybe waiting, for a SLAE scenario to occur.

Whether we realize it or not, we are all Preppers to some extent. For example, children join organizations such as the Boy Scouts or Girl Scouts to better understand nature and learn survival skills. We go grocery shopping to insure we have food for breakfast, lunch, and dinner before we need it. You save money for a "rainy day." You get the point. Whether you are an individual, or part of a family or group, you must determine what it means to be prepared and what you're preparing for.

My family is prepared to live self-sustained for approximately six to twelve months. We're not preparing for a TEOTWAWKI (The End of the World As We Know It) situation. Instead, we're focused on an event such as a tornado, earthquake, hurricane, flood, economic crisis, or H1N1 epidemic—basically anything that would have a mass effect on society with severe repercussions. In most instances, six months to a year should be more than enough time for electricity, food, water, and other essential services to be restored. This was demonstrated by the 2011 tsunami in Japan, in which case the basics necessary for life were restored within months—although the long-term effects of that disaster remain to be seen.

This handbook contains my direct experience and advice. I present examples of portable, fixed, short-term, long-term, expensive, and inexpensive items, theories, and talking points. From these options, you can choose the ones that are best for you. What works for my family and me may or may not work for you. I've learned a lot by watching and reading what expert Preppers have to say and recommend. Many of the opinions have been insightful, while others have not. Nevertheless, I have learned enough to position my family well and to provide others with knowledge and insight into what Preppers think and do. This is the growth experience that non-Preppers need.

I do not believe the world is going to end in my lifetime—but if it does, my Prepping will not save our family. If there is a nuclear attack, my preps will do only so much to keep us alive. I prep for circumstances that would have a direct impact on my family for an extended but finite period of time (one to twelve months). Although I can't control the activities of the universe, I am insuring that my family, through God's will, is in the best possible situation should disaster (natural or not) occur.

Ironically, it's not the event (i.e., tornado, flood, tsunami, nuclear fallout, economic collapse, etcetera) that worries me. It's the human race, of course with exceptions, and how people react to a lack of electricity, limited communications, and little to no available gasoline or food. My family experienced the events of 9/11 while living in upstate New York. Right after the Twin Towers fell, people began to panic. Panicked customers overwhelmed Sam's Club and Walmart. Shelves with the basics, such as water and food, were bare within hours. Lines formed at gas pumps, and in one instance the owner of a gas station closed the building and left the pumps on. To use the pumps, you had to have a credit or debit card. People with cash had to try to convince others to allow them to use their credit cards in exchange for cash; in many instances, these individuals were begging. As you can imagine, this led to numerous tense situations because many people were unwilling to accept cash, which had no value at the time. The mass panic caused more and more chaos—and this was in upstate New York, not in New York City itself!

Compare this U.S. reaction to that of the Japanese following the tsunami of 2011. I have read articles and watched videos of the survivors. There was no panic, no chaos. The Japanese citizens knew that help was on the way and that panicking would only worsen the situation. As they remained calm, housing shelters, first-aid stations, and relief supplies were organized, delivered, and distributed. Everyone was taken care of in an orderly and timely manner. In contrast, following many natural events in the United States, Americans have become violent, selfish, and desperate within a short period of time. Because of 9/11, I realized that I needed to change my life to one where I was more proactive and prepared. This is when I began my journey to becoming a Prepper.

Prepping does and will provide comfort. During a disaster, economic downturn, or other major event you will have peace of mind knowing your preparations will sustain you and your family for a period of time, while others panic or become concerned about survival. Prepping is not something that happens overnight, or even in a year. Prepping is an ongoing lifestyle that must be adapted to the current state of the world. Adapt your Prepping to your budget and circumstances. For example, the chapter on couponing will help you economically begin your Prepping life. Some Preppers spend a lot of money in a short period of time, while others spend little amounts here and there, accumulating what they need over time. Don't be scared, don't panic, just prepare.

Being mentally prepared for a SLAE situation is key to survival. It does no good to have stored food that you're not mentally ready to eat because you think it tastes terrible. It does no good to prep if you're not mentally ready to deal with natural or man-made events, and you freak out. It does no good to prepare for a SLAE scenario if you're not willing to act when required. Are you mentally ready to defend your family or kill a deer for food? Are you ready to provide the emotional support that others will need in a time of crisis? Are you willing to defend your family as well as others who are in your survival group?

In addition to being mentally ready, you must be physically fit. If you're not physically fit, you won't be able to carry out the tasks that will be required in a world without electricity. If you had to, could you walk ten, twenty, or even fifty miles without having a heart attack? Could you carry two five-gallon containers of water for a mile? You don't have to be the Hulk, but you do need to be ready to do more manual work than you did when times were good.

In a world crisis, the elderly, sick, and weak will be the most vulnerable. They will not receive the help they need, which may include food, water, heat, and medical attention. Emergency services will be needed everywhere at once, which is simply not feasible. Once the sick and weak run out of medication, they will no longer have access to additional supplies. Those who depend on electricity for medical equipment will be in an especially difficult situation. Once the power grid shuts down, their medical equipment will no longer function. Immediate panic will be the result. Hospitals will be overrun with people in need. Lines will form, and medical staff will have limited resources. Soon, law enforcement will arrive on the scene to provide protection and preserve order. **You need to be prepared.** Don't be one of those who panics, becomes confused, and must depend on others for survival.

Okay, it's time for the legal stuff. As you read through this book, please understand that it is intended for educational purposes only. My statements should not be used as, or in place of, medical advice. I have communicated with experts and conducted extensive research on the topics in this book, and I have had personal experience with most of the information I present. Nevertheless, I provide this information strictly for your reference and consideration. My goal is to share my journey from not being prepared to being prepared.

¹To every [thing there is] a season, and a time to every purpose under the heaven:
²A time to be born, and a time to die; a time to plant, and a time to pluck up [that which is] planted;
³A time to kill, and a time to heal; a time to break down, and a time to build up;
⁴A time to weep, and a time to laugh; a time to mourn, and a time to dance;
⁵A time to cast away stones, and a time to gather stones together; a time to embrace, and a time to refrain from embracing;
⁶A time to get, and a time to lose; a time to keep, and a time to cast away;
⁷A time to rend, and a time to sew; a time to keep silence, and a time to speak;
⁸A time to love, and a time to hate; a time of war, and a time of peace.

ECCLESIASTES CHAPTER 3 (KJV)

The Theory of Prepping

To better understand Prepping, it must first be distinguished from homesteading and off-grid living. Homesteading was originally a government program under the Homestead Act of 1862, whereby pioneers could settle on a piece of land. As long as homesteaders could improve the land, farm it, and make a profit, ownership would eventually be theirs. This process typically took several years.

Today homesteading is a philosophy with the goal of creating self-sufficiency. "It's about using less energy, eating wholesome local food, involving your family in the life of the community, and making wiser choices that will improve the quality of life for your family, your community, and the environment around you. With today's advanced technology, living off the grid doesn't mean going without electricity, but producing your own with photovoltaics (PV), hydropower, or wind turbines. In addition, home businesses are no longer limited to farm produce stands and craft sales, but can include marketing a home business or telecommuting via the Internet" (Hunt, 2008). Homesteading activities include canning, growing organic food, keeping livestock, and producing energy via solar, wind, geothermal, hydroelectric, or other technologies.

A second form of modern homesteading is urban homesteading, in which people living in the city practice self-sufficiency by living a simple life. They grow and can vegetables, practice permaculture gardening, compost food to make their own soil, keep chickens or ducks, and use solar energy where possible. The goal is self-sufficiency while living in and enjoying the city.

Off-grid living is similar to homesteading, but it takes self-sufficiency one giant step farther. Off-grid living does not rely on municipal sewer systems, water supplies, natural gas, garbage service, or electrical power. A septic tank takes care of the sewage. Off-grid water sources include wells, cisterns, streams, and rain barrels. Garbage is composted and reused in organic gardens. Electrical sources include generators and other forms of solar, wind, geothermal, and micro-hydro energy.

Now let's compare homesteading and off-grid living with Prepping. The basic theory of Prepping is simple: **to be prepared before a significant event (**

SLAE scenario) occurs. In essence, this is a proactive approach to survival. Just as our ancestors relied on basic primitive skills to hunt and survive, we too in a SLAE scenario will revert back to those same primitive skills to survive. Though we take for granted our food sources, grocery stores, computers for online shopping, and restaurants, we will be required to revert to those primitive skills to satisfy the basic needs of survival. As humans our goal is to survive, regardless of the scenario, and to sustain the population as best we can. This is where Prepping comes in. Prepping is not unique. It does involve elements of homesteading and off-grid living. In many cases, Preppers are actively pursuing an ultimate goal of off-grid living or 100 percent self-sufficiency. However, Prepping at its most basic is simply being prepared for an unknown event that will have a direct impact on you, your family, or your group. Remember, Prepping is something you do over time. You don't have to do it overnight.

To prepare effectively, you need to gain the support of your spouse, partner, or family. Prepping is a life-changing philosophy that many people have never heard of or considered. When I started Prepping, I did not have the support of my spouse, and it was extremely difficult. She knew little to nothing about what I was doing—and, frankly, neither did I. In her own words, she thought I was nuts. At first she saw my purchases as wasteful and not practical. When I received stoves, MREs, and other types of survival supplies in the mail, she could not fathom ever having to use the equipment. I had to slowly ease her into the idea and not come on strong or discuss doomsday scenarios. At first the idea was overwhelming for her. She didn't understand why we had to prepare for something that might not happen. She was content doing the weekly shopping, which simply carried us through until her next trip to the grocery store. However, as she became more cognizant of natural disasters across the country, she was able to relate to what I was doing. She saw how important it was to have water, food, heat, and protection. In essence, she had to define Prepping for herself. Now she's actively involved in Prepping, and she makes recommendations on what and when to buy items for our preps. Prepping gives my wife peace of mind as a mother and wife. She is a Prepper in her own right as well as the wife of a Prepper.

As a family, we started out slowly due to limited resources, but now even our children understand the concept of Prepping. We explain why we prep, and they watch how we prep. They actively engage us in questions. Frankly, they love the fact that they can go to our preps and "shop" for any of the five brands of cereal we have.

The following questions may be useful as you discuss prepping with your spouse, partner, family, or friends and attempt to gain their support:

- What does Prepping mean to you?
- What do you know about Prepping?
- Do you feel it's important for us to be prepared?
- What are some of the steps we should take together to prepare? (start small with this one)
- What does Prepping mean to our children?
- How can we/I help our children to understand Prepping?
- What kinds of events do you think we should be prepared for (e.g., earthquake, economic collapse, etc.)?

20He that handleth a matter wisely shall find good:
and whoso trusteth in the LORD, happy is he.
PROVERBS 16:20 (KJV)

3.....man doth not live by bread only.....
DEUTERONOMY 8:3 (KJV)

The Tenets of Prepping

First Tenet: The Survival Triangle

The Prepping community recognizes several tenets, the first of which is the survival triangle.

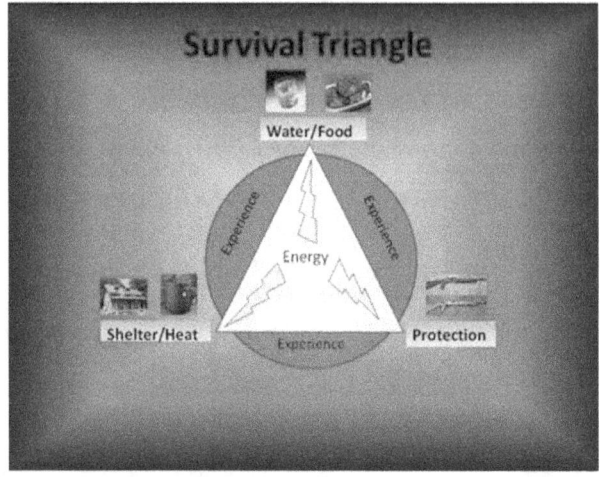

The survival triangle illustrates that, in order to be properly prepared, you must have the elements of all three corners (water/food, shelter/heat, and protection) as well as energy and the experience to utilize your preps. Thus, survival depends on five elements: water/food, shelter/heat, protection, energy, and experience.

Without water or food, it won't matter if you have shelter and heat or protection. The reason is simple. You need water for many reasons, such as to stay hydrated, cook, bathe, brush your teeth, care for animals, and grow plants, to name a few. In the human body, water helps to regulate body temperature (through sweat), protects the nervous system, keeps the skin moist, rids the body of waste, and cushions the joints. On a daily basis, humans need to replace approximately two and a half quarts of water. Either drinking water or eating foods high in water content accomplishes this. Food provides the protein and nutrition necessary to produce energy within the body and sustain life. In addition, food provides nutrients that help to keep our bones, hair, nails, and skin strong and flexible. In a SLAE situation, food can even be used to trade or barter for other necessities.

Without shelter and heat, you won't survive a harsh winter, regardless of the food, water, or protection you have. Shelter keeps you warm in cold weather and dry in the rain. Your shelter also protects your preparations and provides psychological comfort (think "home sweet home"). Your shelter is a place where you can rest your body. Your shelter can protect you from disease (via quarantine) and other threats, whether human, animal, natural, cosmic, and so forth. Heat has a direct impact on many things, including the human body, food stores, and water stores. The most important aspect of heat is its effect on the human body. The body regulates its temperature (98.6° F) to keep all its systems functioning correctly. The balance between body fluids and warmth is both critical and fragile. Remember that the human body is approximately 65 percent water. Dr. Jeffrey Utz, M.D., notes that babies have the most water (78 percent), followed by one-year-old children (65 percent), then adult men (60 percent), and women (55 percent). (Unknown, 2011). Basically, the colder your body temperature, the colder the fluids within your body, and therefore the more likely hypothermia or other serious conditions will occur.

Protection enables you to defend your shelter, water, and food. It also allows you to hunt and exchange for goods or services. Without protection, you and your family or group may become a target for others who can easily take your goods.

Energy is required throughout the survival triangle. When I talk about energy, I do not necessarily mean electricity—although electricity greatly simplifies several components of the triangle if you have a means to produce it (such as a generator or solar, wind, or hydroelectric technology). Primary sources of energy for the Prepper can include propane (in quantities ranging from thousand-gallon tanks to one-pound bottles), wood, batteries, steam, and the previously mentioned generators and solar, wind, or hydroelectric technology.

Finally, you must have experience in survival techniques. If you've never shot a gun, you'll find it difficult in a SLAE situation to protect your shelter or hunt for food; at best, you'll blindly aim and hope for the best. If you don't have experience cooking the food you store, you won't know how to cook it at all, let alone cook it to taste. If you've never learned to filter and purify water found in nature, you could get sick from drinking that water. If you've never learned to repair a shelter or use alternative heat sources, you could be in for some long, cold nights.

Second Tenet: Redundancy

The second tenet of Prepping is redundancy. Redundancy means making sure you have alternative or multiple capabilities for each corner of the survival triangle. Let's take heat for an example. If you lose electricity in the middle of the winter in Wisconsin, how will you stay warm? You might say to yourself, "I have a natural gas heater. I'll be fine." But how will you power the furnace blower without electricity? One alternative could be to have a wood-burning stove with an abundant supply of wood. A second option would be to use a propane heater such as a torpedo heater or a Big Buddy. These units are relatively compact in size but can heat a twelve-hundred-square-foot area comfortably. In addition, they can connect to a thirty-pound propane tank or to one-pound cylinders purchased through major retailers (e.g., Walmart). A third option would be to purchase a kerosene heater with extra wicks and enough kerosene to carry you for two or three weeks. The point is that if one source fails, you should have multiple backup technologies, albeit some simple, to solve the problem.

¹⁷Thou shalt not covet thy neighbour's house, thou shalt not covet thy neighbour's wife, nor his manservant, nor his maidservant, nor his ox, nor his ass, nor any thing that is thy neighbour's.

Exodus 20:17 (KJV)

Third Tenet: Forming a Community

The third tenet of Prepping is to take care of yourself and your family or group. This is the reason you prepare in the first place. In a true SLAE situation we can only take shelter in place so long before outsiders find us and our supplies. Thus we need to partner with our neighbors, friends, or other individuals who prepare as we do. In these groups we learn a new way of life. It is possibly a life based not on money (if there has been an economic collapse) but on the barter and group system, in which we

23

trade our expertise (e.g., construction, plumbing, chemistry, forestry, etcetera) or our goods (e.g., silver, hardware, food, water, etcetera) for what we need. These small groups will provide protection to all individuals but will expect you to do the same. Individuals will be accepted into these groups as they demonstrate the value they bring through their skills and use of those skills. The premise behind this tenant is that you need to reach out to others before others reach out to you, because those others might not reach out in a positive way. You will read this theme several times throughout the book. You need to be integrated and connected with other Preppers or individuals who want to partner and support each other during a SLAE scenario.

Because community is critical to survival, I have developed a relationship with a community of other Preppers. Our group consists of fewer than twenty people, but we form a tight-knit community. Within the community are multiple disciplines and experiences, including mechanical and electrical engineering, architecture, law enforcement, iron- and woodworking, construction, and cooking. Most of the community members are retired, hence the experience, and support of one another. Remember that the individuals within a community are still individuals. Even though they support the group, they will always take care of themselves first. That is simply human nature.

As a beginning Prepper I had a hard time finding other Preppers with whom I wanted to share and learn from. The reason is that my perception was that others would see me as a whacko, or worse, deranged. I was also concerned if others knew my belief it would jeopardize my professional career. For those Preppers who feel as I do, it makes it even more difficult, as it's a double-edged sword. As I tried to keep my anonymity I had to divulge enough information to continue to grow within the Prepper community and expand my network. I came to put everything in perspective and realize that everyone prepares for something. What I prepare for is no different than when my wife prepares dinner. She buys the food one week in advance and in the right amounts. When she needs it, it's there ready to be used. In simplistic terms, this was what I was doing. To form your community or become a part of one, there are many great tools, such as YouTube, Facebook, blogs, and websites. In my experience I've learned that you must first be accepted by an individual or individuals within the community. In my case it was the online community. Specifically, a well-known Prepper on YouTube reached out to me, and hence my network was created. There are also local forums on the internet that are specific to each county in each state; these are a good place to start. There are podcasts such as the *Survival Podcast* by Jack Spirko, which provides excellent information. Remember that the online prepping community doesn't necessarily have an open door, but at the same time it's not closed. You simply have to reach out, and the community will reach back.

"Silence is Golden"
Thomas Carlyle, Sartor Resartus

Fourth Tenet: Silence

The fourth tenet of Prepping is silence. At first it may seem to be in direct conflict with the third tenet of Prepping, but upon further understanding you will see that it is not. The fourth tenet simply means that you must be extremely selective in deciding whom to talk to about your Prepping. The more you divulge about yourself and your preparations, the more you expose yourself. In a SLAE situation individuals will remember your discussions and recall your provisions. Soon they will turn to you for food/water, heat/shelter, and protection. Before you know it, you'll be feeding, protecting, and sheltering non-Preppers en masse, who will come to expect it. Once you stop feeding, protecting, and sheltering them, individuals or gangs may pay you a visit—but not to say hello. In this case, the less information to others the better. The premise is that you may volunteer or be called upon to take care of others if and when possible, but you want to position yourself such that others don't come to you but you go to them. I argue that Preppers should share knowledge and train others. This allows for the greater good of all as more and more people become self-sufficient. It's incumbent that Preppers teach others the basic principles of Prepping and survival. This is why I encourage Preppers and non-Preppers alike to reach out, establish relationships, grow networks, and better understand Prepping and survival skills. Prepping is a delicate balance of self-preservation, helping others where possible, expanding your network, and maintaining privacy.

In the following chapters, I will discuss each element of the survival triangle and explain how and what Preppers may consider to prepare for the unknown in a SLAE and WROL.

Water

A s indicated by the survival triangle, without
water and food your heat, shelter, and protection are in jeopardy. Surviving a SLAE situation is
all about health and getting the proper hydration
and nutrition. The typical rule of thumb is that a
human can survive three minutes without air, three
hours without shelter (i.e. a subzero winter), three
days without water, and three weeks without food.

The average human body is 65 percent water.
To maintain that level, a minimum of two quarts of
water is required per person per day. If you live in a
hot climate, double that to four quarts of water per
person per day. After twenty-four hours without water, dehydration can set in. Symptoms of dehydration
include dry or sticky mouth, an inability to produce

tears, little to no urine output, lethargy, and sunken eyes, according to the National Institutes of Health. Without water, the ability to breathe becomes much more difficult. Lung function uses up to one pint of water every day, decreasing the body's moisture level through exhalation.

In any survival situation, finding clean, drinkable water should be the number-one priority. As a Prepper following the survival triangle, you will have already stored a limited amount of water, but what happens when that is no longer available? **You must find alternative sources of water.**

It's important to understand how water is classified. Potable water is water of sufficiently high quality that it can be consumed with a low risk of immediate or long-term harm. Non-potable water is water that is not of drinkable quality and therefore is not for consumption. In a SLAE situation, there may be times when non-potable water is the only source available. It will be your job to turn this water into safe, potable water. Many of the water sources listed below will require some form of filtration and/or purification prior to drinking.

Sources

There are many sources of water to consider, from the simple to the complex. Some will be on high ground, while others will be on lower ground. Some will be potable, while others are non-potable. Some will provide large quantities of water, while others will provide very little water. Some will provide water in a different form, such as snow, while others will offer water that is difficult to capture, such as condensation. Whatever the source, it's water—and once filtered and purified it will save your life.

First, consider the water in your shelter and/or bug-out location (BOL). A shelter is your primary residence, while a bug-out location is a separate location or place (e.g., house, underground shelter, cave, etcetera) that is available and stocked for use in a SLAE situation. Both locations will have stored water in various quantities. Access to this water is easy, and you know it's potable. Additional sources of water in your shelter or BOL can include a water heater and, yes, a toilet. The water heater is easy to access and easy to drain. A typical hot-water heater will provide anywhere from twenty to eighty gallons of water. A toilet, on the other hand, will provide only about one to six gallons of water, including what's in the tank or cistern. Toilet water must be brought to a rolling boil or treated with chemicals, as discussed in the section titled "Filtration and Purification." Finally, consider that water can be found in the pipes running throughout your house. To gain access to the water in the cold-water pipes, simply open the lowest cold-water faucet in your shelter. If your shelter has more than one floor, the lowest faucet will be found on the first floor or in the basement. You then need to allow air into the pipes to allow for proper drainage. To allow air to enter the cold-water pipes, you will need to open the highest cold-water faucet in your shelter. To gain access to the water in your hot-water pipes, follow the same instructions.

Water can also be found in canned foods, including soups, vegetables, and fruits. When you eat these stores, *never* discard the water; either drink it immediately or store it for later use.

If you live in a cold climate, you may have access to snow. However, snow as a source of water is only a good choice if it's from a relatively clean source of water. Don't eat snow or ice directly, as it will lower your body temperature and potentially lead to dehydration. Instead, heat the snow or ice to melt it.

Rain is a great source of water in many locations. To store rainwater, you first have to capture it. Some options for capturing rainwater include rain barrels positioned to catch water from a house's gutters, containers left on the lawn, tarps funneling water to a container, or an inflatable children's pool. In the forest, rain is often trapped on leaves and within plants.

If you live in an area with a high water table, you can simply dig until you hit ground water or surface water. This is hard work, but the payoff will save your life. Prior to drinking this water, you will need to find a way to capture and store it. Then you must filter the water as discussed in the section titled "Filtration and Purification."

Wells are another great source of water; however, you must remember to have a manual pump in the event that electricity is not available. Wells typically tap into an aquifer, which is basically an underground lake.

Cisterns are watertight structures used to store water. Most often the water found in a cistern comes from rain.

Surface water, such as lakes and rivers, provides an excellent source. Once again, however, the water is only as good as the source. In all instances, I would highly recommend purifying surface water prior to drinking it. The last section of this chapter is entirely devoted to various means of filtering and purifying water.

Condensation is a rather difficult source of water simply because it's hard to capture. Condensation occurs when the temperature of the air equals the dew-point temperature. The dew point is the temperature at which water vapor begins to condensate. Condensation forms when there are extreme temperature changes between day and night. One method of capturing condensation is to use a metal roof with an incline. Simply place a container or bucket underneath the roof to catch the water.

An underground solar still can be constructed as an additional source of water, although in most cases it will not provide the volume of water required for a family. Simply search the internet for "underground still" to find many useful articles and websites.

Water can also be purchased in a pouch or a boxed water kit. Depending on the vendor, this water may meet United States Coast Guard standards and, based on packaging, have an extended shelf life.

Liquids Not to Consume

In any situation where water is scarce, there are several liquids that should **not** be consumed at any time. First, and contrary to popular belief, **do not** drink urine. Urine is excreted from your body for a reason. It is 95 percent water, but the remaining 5 percent is **waste** that includes urea, dissolved salts, and organic compounds. Don't drink it. Second, never drink alcohol. Alcohol is a diuretic, which is the reason you urinate so much while drinking. Because of the frequent urination and lack of water you become dehydrated and get that classic hangover headache. Third, don't drink coffee. It's another diuretic that causes you to urinate frequently and can lead to dehydration. Other natural diuretics include apple cider vinegar, green tea, cranberry juice, asparagus, oats, lettuce, and cabbage—but eaten in small quantities, these should cause no concern about dehydration.

Storage

You typically need a minimum of one gallon of water per person per day. Let's say you plan to store a one-month supply of water for a family of five. In this case, you would need 150 gallons of water (thirty days multiplied by five family members equals 150 gallons). How would you store 150 gallons of water, and where would you store it?

How much water you can store will depend on four things:

- the amount of storage you have,
- how you organize your storage area,
- how you store your water, and
- what your mobility is (for example, will you be moving water from your shelter to your vehicle as you move locations?).

Remember, water is heavy. It weighs about 8.35 pounds per gallon. If you shelter in place, your storage conditions will be different than if you're in your bug-out vehicle (BOV) headed to your bug-out location (BOL). In other words, storing water in a house is different than storing water in a moving vehicle. One helpful feature of water is that it takes the shape of its container. I would use this feature to your advantage. For example, water stored in a hundred-gallon Water-Bob (which costs less than twenty dollars) will assume the shape of the bathtub or other location in which it's stored. If possible, it's best to store your water in a cool, dark location such as a basement.

The most cost-effective way to store water is by recycling your milk, juice, and similar jugs. We simply wash them out and fill them with filtered water from our Berkey. A Berkey is gravity water-filtration unit. Other means of water storage include but are not limited to the following:

- Seven- to fifty-five-gallon food-grade containers/barrels inside your shelter for water storage
  - A fifty-five-gallon barrel full of water weighs approximately 450 pounds, so it must be placed in a location from which you have no plans of moving it unless you have a dolly.
- Fifty-five-gallon food-grade barrels outside your shelter to capture rainwater
  - This water will need to be filtered and purified as previously discussed.

○ Water stored outdoors may freeze in the winter, depending on your location, so the barrels will need to be emptied and stored during this time of year. Keep in mind that with your rainwater barrels emptied and stored you have decreased your water stores by fifty-five gallons per barrel, and you will need to replace that water by other storage means.

- WaterBobs
  ○ These fit conveniently in your bathtub and hold up to one hundred gallons of water. They are inexpensive and a great item to have in your preps.

The WaterBob was designed for emergency drinking-water storage. It's meant to be placed in your bathtub and has a capacity of up to one hundred gallons.

Filtration and Purification

As indicated before, your water may require filtration prior to consumption. Depending on the source of your water, it may contain particles such as wood, leaves, mud, and rocks that need to be filtered out. The simplest and most effective means of filtering water is to use cheesecloth or coffee filters. In a survival situation, use your clothes. The goal is to remove as many of the big particles as possible. If the water is muddy or cloudy, let it sit for up to twelve hours; then slowly ladle or remove the water without disturbing any material that may have settled to the bottom of the container.

Next you must purify your water. In order to understand the importance of purifying water, it's helpful to know why it needs to be purified. Water contains pathogens, or infectious agents. Two common pathogens found in water are cryptosporidium (sometimes called crypto) and giardia. Cryptosporidiosis is a parasitic disease that affects the intestines. Cryptosporidium causes diarrhea, which can lead to dehydration if not carefully watched. Symptoms of cryptosporidiosis typically occur two to ten days after ingestion and last for a few weeks. Cryptosporidium can only be killed by bringing water to a rolling boil. It is highly resistant to chlorine treatment; therefore, chemical disinfectants have been shown not to be 100 percent effective in killing it.

Giardia is another parasite that affects the small intestines. Symptoms often appear one to two weeks after ingestion and include, but are not limited to, diarrhea (watch out for dehydration), stomach cramps, nausea, and an upset stomach. These symptoms can last anywhere from one to two weeks. The Centers for Disease Control and Prevention states that "to kill or inactivate giardia, bring your water to a rolling boil for one minute (at elevations above 6,500 feet, boil for three minutes). Water should then be allowed to cool, stored in a clean sanitized container with a tight cover, and refrigerated" (*Prevention*, 2006).

Bringing water to a rolling boil per the CDC guidelines is the best way to eradicate both cryptosporidium and giardia and to insure the safety of your drinking water. In addition, this method of purification is highly cost-effective (starting a fire in nature to boil water is essentially free).

Other water diseases and/or pathogens include but are not limited to the following:

- Dysentery
- Typhoid
- E. coli
- Salmonella
- Hepatitis
- Rotavirus
- Norovirus (formerly Norwalk)

Once again, boiling is the most effective means of purifying water. However, there are other effective means, which include both chemicals and filters to eliminate pathogens. Chemical means of water purification include the following:

- Potassium permanganate
  - ° This is another cheap and easy way to purify water. Potassium permanganate crystals can be bought at hardware stores. Add three or four crystals per quart of water (or until the water stains a light pink) and let the water sit for thirty minutes.
  - ° Water treated with potassium permanganate can also be used as a disinfectant for cleaning wounds. Simply add crystals one by one until the water turns pink. You need a solution of approximately 0.01 percent, which requires about three or four crystals per quart of water.
- Chlorine bleach
  - ° This can also be a cheap and effective means of purifying water. The Washington State Department of Health has created the following guidelines (Health W. S., 2011):

Treating Water with a 5-6 Percent Liquid Chlorine Bleach Solution		
Volume of Water to be Treated	Treating Clear/Cloudy Water: Bleach Solution to Add	Treating Cloudy, Very Cold, or Surface Water: Bleach Solution to Add
1 quart/1 liter	3 drops	5 drops
1/2 gallon/2 quarts/2 liters	5 drops	10 drops
1 gallon	1/8 teaspoon (approximately 10 drops)	1/4 teaspoon
5 gallons	1/2 teaspoon	1 teaspoon
10 gallons	1 teaspoon	2 teaspoons

- ° **Wait one hour before drinking water treated with chlorine bleach.**
- Tincture of iodine (2 percent)
  - ° Pregnant or nursing women or anyone with a thyroid condition should not use this method. If the water is mostly clear, use four drops of iodine per quart of water (sixteen drops of iodine per gallon). If the water is cloudy, and you were unable to filter the water, use eight drops of iodine per quart (thirty-two drops per gallon).
  - ° **Wait one hour before drinking water treated with tincture of iodine.**
- Purification tablets
  - ° These typically contain either iodine or chlorine and should be used according to the manufacturer's instructions.
- Calcium hypochlorite
  - ° Also called pool shock or HTH (high-test hypochlorite), this chemical is often used in swimming pools. **Make sure you purchase "pure" calcium hypochlorite (65 to 70 percent grade) that contains no other chemicals (e.g., clarifiers, anti-fungals, etcetera).**

° Filter your water as discussed previously. Then follow these guidelines from the U.S. Army Center for Health Promotion and Preventive Medicine to make a diluted solution of calcium hypochlorite. You will add this solution to your main water supply to disinfect it. **Do not drink the solution itself**.

1. Place one heaping tablespoon of calcium hypochlorite in two gallons of water and wait for it to dissolve.

2. Once it's dissolved, add the solution you just made to your main supply of water to disinfect it. The suggested ratio is one part chlorine solution to one hundred parts water. This is equivalent to one pint of solution for every twelve and a half gallons of water (eight pints equals one gallon).

3. Store any remaining calcium hypochlorite material (i.e., what's left in the package) in a cool, dry place.

Non-chemical means of purification include but are not limited to the following:

• Filtration units such as the Berkey, the AquaRain Natural Water Filter, and the MSR Autoflow Gravity Water Filter.

Berkeys come in different sizes and are phenomenal at filtering water from different sources, including tap water, wells, rivers, lakes, and rainwater.

- Hand-pump filters such as the MiniWorks EX Hand Pump Filter and the Katadyn Mini Ultralight Water Filter

- Millbanks bags. These bags made of closely woven canvas are used to pre-filter water with heavy sediment and were developed for U.S. forces during World War II. Using a Millbanks bag in conjunction with chemical sterilization can make even the most heavily silted water safe and palatable to drink. A Millbanks bag will also prolong the life of a microporous ceramic filter if used as a pre-filter.

MiniWorks EX Hand Pump Filter

- Microfiltration water filters. These remove contaminants by passing water through a membrane. An example is the Katadyn Pocket filter. The output of the Katadyn Pocket filter is up to one quart per minute, and it can filter up to thirteen thousand gallons, depending on water quality.

Survival straws. These use a highly efficient water purification system to destroy the harmful bacteria and viruses that exist in most sources of water. Unlike a typical filter that attempts to trap impurities, the survival straw eliminates them. Some manufacturers claim that a single survival straw can process over five thousand gallons of water, although I cannot verify this claim. As the names implies, a survival straw is used in the same manner a regular straw is used. You place the straw directly in the water and drink. The water is purified as it passes through the purification substrate.

[8]Remove far from me vanity and lies: give me neither poverty nor riches; feed me with food convenient for me:

PROVERBS 30:8 (KJV)

Food

On average, a person can go three weeks without food. Factors that will have a direct impact on how long you can go without food include the following:

- your health,
- your metabolism,
- your ratio of body fat to muscle,
- your hydration level,
- the temperature of your environment, and
- the work you are performing.

Every Prepper must determine what foods to store, how to store them, and how much is necessary. Regardless of the type and quantity of food you store, you must remember to store what you eat and eat what you store. This is called rotating your food supply. Not everyone follows this practice. I know individuals who purchase food they do not intend to use unless there is a SLAE situation. This is truly a disadvantage, as you may not know how to cook with the food you've stored, let alone enjoy the taste.

There are two types of food supplies: short-term and long-term. Short-term foods supplies typically last three days to a month and are high in protein and calories. I use Meals-Ready-to-Eat (MREs) for my short-term food source. They are self-contained, ready to eat, and high in calories. The purpose of your long-term food supplies is to feed you and your family for up to six months, with one year being the goal for most Preppers. Keep in mind that as you store food, make sure you monitor the expiration date. Some foods are good for months, while others are good for up to thirty years, depending on storage conditions. To achieve the longest storage times possible, your food supplies need to be stored in a cool, dry space (approximately 70° F). In addition, they need to be protected from rodents such as mice and rats.

Preservation

Food preservation is the process of stopping or slowing down spoilage in order to allow for longer storage. Foods that are not properly stored quickly lose their nutritional value and taste, and they can even become inedible.

Preservation involves preventing the growth of microorganisms such as bacteria and fungi, as well as the oxidation of fats. In the following pages I describe several methods of food preservation.

One common technique for preserving and storing food involves the use of five- to six-gallon food-grade buckets, Mylar bags, desiccants, and oxygen absorbers. It is especially useful for storing bulk items such as rice, wheat, or legumes. Because of its popularity, effectiveness, and low cost I will describe the process in some detail:

- Preheat a steam iron (with steam off) on the hottest available setting (usually "Linen" or "Cotton"). In order to properly seal the Mylar bag, the iron's temperature needs to be at or near 400° F.
- Remove the lid from your food-grade pail and place the Mylar bag in the pail.
  ○ For a five- to six-gallon pail, place one or two one-ounce packets of desiccant in the bottom of the Mylar bag prior to filling it with food.
  ○ Pour your food (e.g., wheat, beans, rice, etcetera) into the Mylar bag.
  ○ Place an oxygen absorber on top of the grain or beans.

- ° Fold the top of the Mylar bag as close to the food as you can.
- ° Place a flat object under the fold and then seal the Mylar bag by ironing across the fold.
- ° Replace the lid of the pail and store it in a cool, dry location.

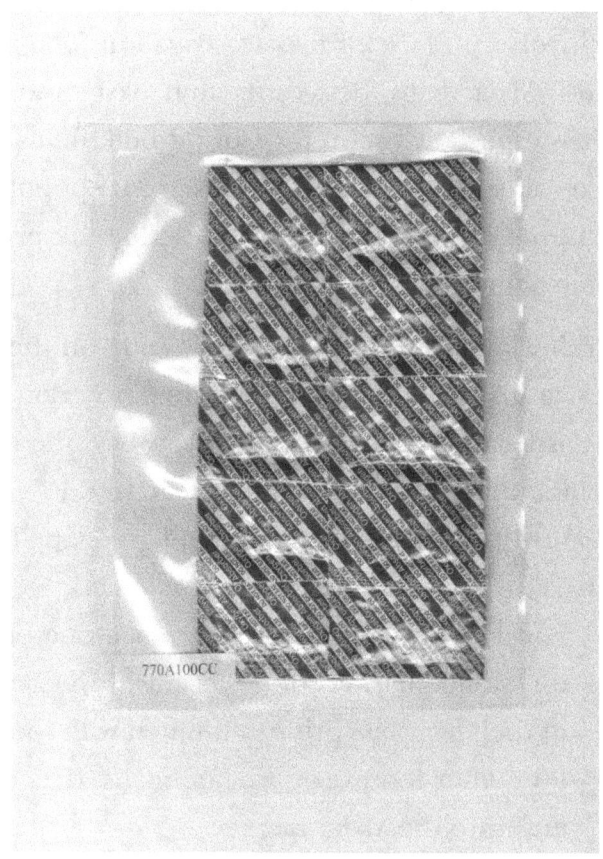

770A100CC

Oxygen absorbers

Some other methods of preserving food include the following:

- Freezing
  - Most foods can be preserved by storing them in a freezer set at 0° F. Provided that you don't have to buy a freezer, and you have storage room, this is a cost-effective method of storage and preservation. You need to be prepared should electricity not be available. What will you do with this food?
  - The National Center for Food Preservation (Harison, 2006) states that storage containers for freezer use should not become brittle or crack at low temperatures. They should be the following:
    - resistant to moisture vapor,
    - durable and leak proof,
    - resistant to oil, grease, and water,
    - able to protect foods from absorbing flavors or odors,
    - easy to seal, and
    - easy to mark.
- Canning
  - Either a water or a pressure canning method can be used to inhibit the growth of microorganisms, yeast, and mold. In the canning

process, each jar forms a vacuum seal to protect food and to prevent oxygen from entering.

- ° Upfront costs for canning include jars, lids, a pressure cooker or hot-water bath, and a few canning tools. Stores typically put canning equipment on sale at the end of the summer, but used canning supplies can often be found at garage sales for an extremely reasonable price.

- ° Pickling, or brining, is a process of preserving food (e.g., cucumber pickles) by fermentation in a salt solution. The food is typically stored in an acidic solution (e.g., 5 percent vinegar) that destroys most bacteria.

- Vacuum sealing
  - ° A vacuum sealer can be used to remove air from a bag or container. Without oxygen, microbes are unable to form. Vacuum sealing can be used in conjunction with other preservation methods.

  - ° Upfront costs for this method include the vacuum sealer and plastic bags. The purchase of additional plastic bags, which can be specific to a particular brand or model of vacuum sealer, is an ongoing cost.

- Dry-pack method
    - ○ This is the current method of the Latter-Day Saints. It preserves food in #10 steel cans to prevent the growth of microorganisms, yeast, and mold. Oxygen absorbers are used to minimize the amount of air in the can, and the cans are sealed using a dry-pack canning machine. The cans are labeled with the contents and date. They can be stored safely for the longest possible shelf life.

Short-Term Food Supplies

If you are new to Prepping, I highly recommend that you start your journey by establishing a short-term food supply. This gives you experience in understanding what to store, how much to store, and how to store and cook your food preparations (preps). Short-term food supplies are meant to last anywhere from one day to a month, and they most definitely overlap with long-term food supplies. Odds are that these will be foods you eat on a regular basis as compared to the long-term foods listed below.

Keep in mind that water is always your first priority. If water supplies are a concern, avoid storing food and drinks with a high salt content. The more salt you consume, the more water you will want to drink. Also, as mentioned previously, avoid diuretics such as beer and coffee unless you have a large water reserve.

Foods high in protein are essential for both short-term and long-term storage. In fact, many of the foods you use for short-term storage will also be used in your long-term storage, but in much greater quantities. Whenever possible, store food in single servings or family-size servings to avoid leftovers since refrigeration may not be available. It's important to note that emergency kits are commercially available, but at a much higher cost than do-it-yourself kits. Nevertheless, they can quickly bolster your food supply as well as provide the portability you may require.

Short-term foods include but are not limited to the following:

- Ready-to-eat foods such as MREs (Meals-Ready-to-Eat)
- Dehydrated or freeze-dried fruits and vegetables
- Cookies, candy, or other snacks
- Cereals and crackers
- Smoked or dried meats like beef jerky

See the following list ("Long-Term Food Supplies") for more suggestions.

Long-Term Food Supplies

I classify long-term foods as those that can be stored from five to thirty years, based on storage conditions.

I firmly believe that the best long-term foods are the basics. Often these are not the foods you're used to eating, but through time they have sustained entire cultures. If you don't presently eat the basic foods listed below, you need to start. Learn to cook with them, and include them as part of your normal food rotation. Learn how to grind wheat. Find out how to make bread. Brush up on all the fundamentals of cooking!

The basic foods you should consider include the following:

- Grains
  - These typically store well for ten years, but wheat can last up to twenty years if stored properly. Grains include wheat berries, quinoa, oats, barley, flaxseed, and millet.
- Dried legumes (e.g., soybeans, split peas, and lentils)
  - Properly stored, these can last for seven to ten years.
- Dried fruits and vegetables
  - These can be kept for seven to ten years if properly stored.
- Rice
  - Properly stored, rice can be kept for seven to ten years.

- Corn
  - According to the Federal Emergency Management Administration, (FEMA), dried corn can be stored indefinitely, provided that it is properly stored in appropriate containers and isn't contaminated by insects, moisture, or other environmental contaminants.
- Honey
  - This never spoils.
- Dry milk
  - This will last up to five years if stored properly.

Other long-term foods to consider include the following:
- MREs (Meals-Ready-to-Eat)
  - An MRE is a self-contained, individual field ration in lightweight packaging that the United States military provides for its service members. MREs were designed for use in combat or other field conditions where organized food facilities are not available.
- Freeze-dried foods
  - These can be stored for up to twenty-five years in proper storage conditions.

The freezing process preserves food and other perishable items. Freeze-dried foods weigh less and take up less space than their fresh counterparts, so they are much easier to transport.

- ° Examples include buffalo-style chicken, spaghetti, beef stew, green beans, corn, and beef stroganoff with noodles.
- Dehydrated foods
  - ° Dehydration is a process of food preservation that works by removing water from the food, which inhibits the growth of microorganisms.
  - ° Dehydrated food can be stored for as long as thirty years in proper storage conditions.
  - ° Examples include iodized salt, white flour, cracked wheat cereal, quick oats, rolled oats, buttermilk powder, and peanut butter powder.

When storing food, don't forget items like spices, salt, pepper, vinegar, bouillon cubes, sugar, vegetable oil, shortening, baking powder, baking soda, yeast, and dry soup mixes. These items will help to give your food more flavors and make unfamiliar foods more appealing. Remember to buy what you eat and eat what you buy. In other words, always rotate your food for freshness and shelf life.

Herbs

Herbs should also be included in any Prepper's food stores. Herbs provide a natural means of soothing, maintaining, and healing the human body in addition to making food more flavorful. If the world were to experience a true pandemic, herbs would replace medicine due to its lack of availability. Below are descriptions of the health benefits of some common herbs. This is by no means a complete list. Furthermore, the health benefits listed below are only a sampling of the reasons why you should include herbs in your food preps.

- Basil inhibits the growth of several types of bacteria. It also has anti-inflammatory effects and is a source of vitamin A, vitamin K, calcium, manganese, and magnesium.

- Chamomile acts as a mild relaxant to combat depression, stress, and anxiety. It is also a muscle relaxant, helps the skin in cases of burns and allergies, and works as a sleep aid, cold fighter, and wound healer.

- Cilantro has anti-inflammatory properties, relieves stomach gas, and has protective properties against bacterial infection. It also helps to increase HDL and reduce LDL cholesterol, adds fiber to the digestive tract, detoxifies the body, and contains immune boosting properties.

- Cinnamon basil offers relief from diarrhea, constipation, kidney problems, coughs, headaches, and warts. It is an excellent source of a variety of key nutrients, particularly vitamin C, calcium, vitamin A, and phosphorus. Furthermore, it is a useful source of magnesium, potassium, and iron.
- Dill helps with digestion, cancer prevention (monoterpenes), dysentery, insomnia, diarrhea, and respiratory disorders. It also has anti-congestive and histaminic properties.
- Lemon balm eases pain from cold sores or herpes and offers headache relief. Its sedative properties soothe nervousness from anxiety, improve the memory, alleviate menstruation discomfort, and clear up acne.
- Mint and lemon mint helps prevent cancer (it contains a phytonutrient called perilly alcohol). It also soothes the digestive tract, and its antifungal properties are thought to play a role in the treatment of asthma and other allergy conditions.
- Oregano offers relief from diarrhea, constipation, kidney problems, coughs, headaches, and warts. It is an excellent source of a variety of key nutrients, particularly vitamin C, calcium, vitamin A, and phosphorus. Furthermore, it is a useful source of magnesium, potassium, and iron.

⁹Have not I commanded thee? Be strong and of a good courage; be not afraid, neither be thou dismayed: for the LORD thy God is with thee whithersoever thou goest.

JOSHUA 1:9 (KJV)

Shelter and Heat

Shelter/Bug-Out Location

A shelter is your primary living location, while a bug-out location (BOL) is a house, underground shelter, fifth-wheel trailer, camper, cave, or other place/location that you can use in a SLAE situation; basically, it's a secondary living location. Not all individuals have access to or can afford a BOL.

Should you need to Get out of Dodge (GOOD) a BOL should be available when you need it. The BOL should be stocked with provisions and located within a few hours' drive. It takes more than five hours to drive to my BOL, which means it's not quickly accessible. As such, I have to be prepared at all times with plenty of gas, food, and other supplies.

A BOL does not have to be secluded, such as in the middle of a forest, but it needs to provide and support the elements of the survival triangle. Regardless of its location, your shelter or BOL needs to protect you and your family from rain, snow, wind, sun, rodents, and insects. In addition, it needs to be able to maintain a comfortable temperature as efficiently as possible.

My BOL is in the northern part of the United States. It is situated on a major lake and is surrounded by forest. We have access to fish, bears, deer, geese, rabbits, and other wildlife. The lake could be used for our water source should our well fail. We have multiple means of filtering the lake water to provide clean, healthy water. For shelter we have an older home that is well insulated and situated fifty feet from the lake. The lot is big enough to allow a five-hundred-square-foot garden that would provide fresh vegetables and fruits for canning in the summertime. There is easy access to the forest (within fifty feet) and an almost limitless amount of fuel (i.e., trees). The trees could also be used for building or maintaining structures such as hunting blinds. I wanted a BOL that was fairly close to a major city (approximately one hour away), yet somewhat isolated. This setting works for me but may not work for you. Your BOL could be as simple as grabbing your tent(s) and other supplies and heading to a familiar location that you feel is far enough away from the chaos. A BOL does not have to be elaborate, but it has to provide the safety you would require in a short- or long-term SLAE situation.

Heat

As mentioned previously, redundancy is a critical element in all aspects of Prepping. Heat is no exception. If you live in the northern, Midwestern, or eastern portion of the United States, heat is essential. Without heat, pipes freeze, water freezes, hypothermia sets in, and your life becomes extremely miserable.

In many SLAE situations, electricity is a luxury. This is obviously a problem if your house's primary source of heat is electrical, but a lack of electricity can affect other heat sources as well. For example, if you have natural gas you can continue to generate heat for your shelter, but your fan or blower won't circulate that heat without electricity. Thus, you need to have multiple backup sources of fuel for heat. Backup fuel sources include resources such as wood, newspaper, alcohol, and so on. In addition, there are sources such as jet fuel, unleaded fuel, diesel, propane, kerosene, and even candles. Below I've listed several of my back-up heat sources and fuels and explained why I chose them.

Take, for instance, the Yukon M1950 stove. U.S. soldiers in the Korean War used this stove, and it can now be purchased in military-surplus stores for approximately $170. It is extremely compact when not in use, yet it assembles to provide a fully functional source of heat. This stove can use many types of fuel, including wood, jet fuel, diesel fuel, and unleaded gasoline. The Yukon has a steel body (10 X 24 X 8 in.) and a latched swinging door on one end with a sliding draft gate. When its legs are unfolded, they support the stove approximately 8 ¾ inches off the ground. The stove includes five twenty-three-inch sections of fit-together exhaust pipe, a draft inverter to attach at the top of the exhaust pipes (which would be outside), and guy lines for pipe support. The entire unit weighs only twenty-eight pounds. I can easily pick it up and carry it anywhere, or use it in the house if I need to. It is perfect for both bugging out and sheltering in place.

The Yukon M1950 when assembled and ready to use a solid fuel such as wood.

The Big Buddy is a good example of a propane heat source that can further your redundancy. Mr. Heater's Big Buddy can use propane cylinders in a variety of sizes, from the one-pound cylinders you can buy at Walmart or Target up to and including twenty-pound cylinders. The propane cylinders connect on each side of the Big Buddy (inside the door).

I've used the Big Buddy for some time now, and I like the compactness as well as the BTUs. The Big Buddy has a built-in blower that can circulate heated air for heating efficiency when used indoors. The fan operates on either four D-size batteries or a six-volt A/C adapter. From a safety perspective, the Big Buddy has a low-oxygen shut-off system, tip-over shut-off system, and a heavy-duty safety guard. The Big Buddy has very respectable heating times, as shown in this chart:

Number and Size of Cylinders	Hours of Heating Time
one 1-lb. cylinder	1.5–6 hours
two 1-lb. cylinders	3–12 hours
one 20-lb. cylinder	25–110 hours
two 20-lb. cylinders	50–220 hours

A third form of heating redundancy that I use is a kerosene heater. There are two types of kerosene heaters: convection and radiant. Both types have circular fiberglass wicks that use capillary action to transport the kerosene straight to the burner. In a radiant kerosene heater, the burner is in a glass cylinder that has repellent stainless steel behind it. When you turn on the device, the burner turns red and sends heat waves outward. Radiant kerosene heaters produce some convection heat, but they mostly project the heat forward, to the walls and windows. Convection is simply the movement of the air around the kerosene heater due to a temperature increase. Kerosene can last up to five years if properly stored in approved metal or plastic containers. K-1 kerosene is safe because it burns cleanly, and if you have the wick set properly, it gives off little or no smoke. The kerosene heater is economical in terms of fuel cost. In the Midwest, kerosene heaters run anywhere from fifty dollars to two hundred dollars.

Protection

Once again let's go back to the survival triangle. Without protection, your food, water, shelter, and heat are in jeopardy. The reason is simple: People will react differently in a SLAE situation, but people will *always* look out for themselves and their families. More to the point, people will not act as they did prior to the SLAE, and this will include the relationships they had with other peers, families, groups, and so on. They will do whatever they can to find water and food, obtaining it by any means within their power—up to and including violence. Because of this, many individuals will not have prepared for the situation, and they will want us to give them some or maybe all of our stores or preparations.

It's also critical to remember that not all Preppers are truly prepared; each one has a different goal for, and understanding of, Prepping. For example, some Preppers may only purchase weapons and ammunition. When exposed to a SLAE scenario, they will quickly learn that they're in trouble because they only prepared for the protection corner of the survival triangle. They will discover that without food, water, shelter, and heat they have failed. These Preppers are smart enough to realize that there are other Preppers who are properly and completely prepared. They will seek these individuals out, either in a positive or negative manner, and seek assistance.

When the word *protection* is mentioned, the first thing that comes to mind is firearms. As we all know, firearms come in various sizes, models, prices, and types. In this handbook we will discuss two types of firearms: long guns and pistols.

Shotguns and rifles are the most common types of long guns. Long guns can be either lever action (e.g., Walther Lever Action), pump action (e.g., Winchester Model 6), semiautomatic action (e.g., DPMS Oracle Semi-Automatic 308), hinge action, or bolt action (e.g., Winchester Model 59).

Semiautomatics and revolvers are the most common types of pistols. Pistols are classified as single action, double action, or semiautomatic, as seen in the following:

- Single action. The hammer must be cocked with the thumb prior to releasing the trigger. Most single actions require that the hammer must be cocked each and every time the gun is fired. An example is the Beretta Stampede.
- Double action. The trigger cocks and releases the hammer when released. There are two main ways that double action works. The first way is actually single action, whereby the hammer is cocked with the thumb, and when the trigger is pulled the hammer is tripped. The second way is true double action, whereby you simply pull the trigger, which cocks the hammer, revolves the cylinder, and trips the hammer, thus firing the round. An example is the Ruger Super Redhawk Alaskan.
- Semiautomatic: A single chamber is positioned at the rear of the barrel. A slide moves backward, ejecting the fired case and then pulling another cartridge up from the magazine as it moves forward. An example is the CZ75 Omega.

I recommend having a combination of close-range weapons, long-range weapons, varmint weapons, and weapons that have a wide shot pattern when fired. In a SLAE situation, especially during the early stages, it is unlikely that you'll have a close encounter requiring firearms. Nevertheless, always be prepared. Your goal will be to keep others as far away from your main shelter or BOL as possible. This will be accomplished with your long-range arms. As time progresses and the situation becomes more desperate, you may be faced with a close encounter with an individual or a group. You need to be prepared and to understand that these people are desperate, hungry, and willing to do whatever it takes to fulfill the basic requirements of life.

Other types of protection include tools for detecting any source of danger that may approach your shelter or BOL. You need to be alerted as soon as possible to any danger, day or night. Some tools that provide this capability are briefly described in the following:

- Infrared detectors
  - For example, the MURS Alert Transmitter , which "offers the ability to monitor activity at remote locations. The MURS Alert Transmitter utilizes passive infrared sensor technology that will transmit an alert signal to the MURS Base and Hand Held radio in order to notify you that someone has entered a monitored area" (Unknown)

- ° Offer real-time alerts
- ° Are relatively inexpensive to implement and extremely practical
- ° Can be placed around the perimeter of your BOL for added security
- ° Can be easily concealed, thereby avoiding detection
- Motion detectors
  - ° Can be strategically placed to detect motion
  - ° Are cost effective and provide real-time detection
  - ° Most common motion detectors measure body heat (passive)
- Infrared (IR) game cameras
  - ° Allow images to be seen in low levels of light, approaching total darkness
  - ° Do not provide real-time feedback
  - ° Take photos of images and store them to an internal disk. The disk must be manually reviewed for content
- Closed-circuit television (CCTV)
  - ° Use video cameras to transmit a signal to a specific place, on a predefined set of monitors, and therefore provide real-time observations
  - ° Can be extremely expensive, and unless you plan for its purchase it may not be practical

- ° Can purchase cameras with remote monitoring. With this option you can monitor your shelter anywhere there is a computer connection
- Handheld infrared video recorders
  - ° Provide the capability to see heat signatures (sources) in the dark and therefore provide real-time observations
  - ° Are manually operated, therefore you have to be actively using the recorders to see the heat signatures
  - ° Are moderately expensive but practical
- Night-vision goggles (NVGs)
  - ° Allow images to be seen in levels of light approaching total darkness
  - ° Can be hands free, depending on type
  - ° Offer real-time observations
  - ° Manually operated, therefore you have to be awake
  - ° Moderately expensive but practical
- Binoculars
  - ° Same as night-vision goggles but are limited to daylight use only, unless the IR option is purchased
  - ° Allow you to monitor your property, hunt, or scout from a distance
  - ° Are available in many magnifications
  - ° Price ranges vary, depending on your budget

Energy

Energy is a critical component of each element in the survival triangle. When we think of energy, we automatically think about the electricity that powers our homes, hospitals, and the everyday world. It just shows up, and everything we need is powered. But what happens if there is no electricity? Could you live for three days, three weeks, or three months without electricity? The answer is "probably not," and that's why Preppers need alternative energy sources. In this chapter I will discuss options that allow you to remain in your primary shelter, as well as options that can be used in your BOL. Many of them are practical in terms of cost, while others are quite expensive and therefore less practical for most people. Nevertheless, I will present them all for the purpose of education. Choose the energy options that are right for you and your family.

Solar

- Solar generators
  - A solar-power generator is made up of a few small components that include a battery charger, the generator itself, and the frames. The solar-panel frames on the generator gather and harness the sun's energy and store the

energy in a battery. Most solar generators can store that energy for a very long time, up to a year. The smaller camping versions of solar-power generators are very lightweight and easy to assemble, so they can be moved and taken anywhere. Their portability is a large reason why they are becoming so popular among the public.

- Prices start around twelve hundred dollars.
- Solar panels (portable and fixed)
  - Portable solar-power systems are similar to devices such as battery chargers, backup power generators, and even mobile devices used for wireless system work. These devices are ideal for anyone who travels and is constantly on the go. Different systems provide varying watts to power items like laptops, radios, shortwave radios, and portable lighting.
    - Prices range from below one hundred dollars to thousands of dollars.
  - Fixed solar panels are typically photovoltaic (PV) modules or panels. The module or panel is an assembly of photovoltaic cells or solar cells. These systems are flexible enough to provide electricity for anything from a camper to a commercial application. A single solar panel

will provide only a limited amount of energy; therefore, it may be necessary to purchase or install several panels to meet your energy requirements. Other components that may be required include an inverter and a battery with the appropriate wiring.

- These systems are based on your energy requirements, so prices vary.

Wind

Wind power is the conversion of wind energy into a useful form of energy, such as wind turbines that make electricity, windmills for mechanical power, wind pumps for water pumping or drainage, and sails that propel ships. Wind power, as an alternative to fossil fuels, is plentiful, renewable, widely distributed, and clean, It produces no greenhouse gas emissions. Typical wind-power units are not portable and must be installed to a fixed base. Prices range from about forty-five dollars for a thirty-two watt wind turbine to well over one hundred thousand dollars for a residential system.

Hydro (Water)

Hydropower systems use the energy in flowing water to produce electricity or mechanical energy. Although there are several ways to harness moving water to produce energy, run-of-the-river systems, which do not require large storage reservoirs, are often used for micro-hydropower systems. Hydropower systems require property that has access to flowing water. Most home units utilize micro-hydro turbines connected to an alternator or similar system to produce power. These systems can be pricey, but the payoff is a green technology with the potential of producing unlimited energy.

Geothermal

Geothermal energy uses heat from the interior of the earth. This heat, or thermal energy, originates from the formation of the planet, from the radioactive decay of minerals, and from volcanic activity. Geothermal power is cost effective, reliable, sustainable, and environmentally friendly, but it has historically been limited to areas near tectonic-plate boundaries. Geothermal systems range in price, starting at twenty-five thousand dollars and going up from there.

Wood

Wood is probably humankind's very first source of energy. Today it still is the single most important source of renewable energy, providing over 9 percent of the global primary-energy supply (*Nations*, 2011). Wood energy is as important as all other renewable energy sources together. As previously mentioned, wood is a great source of fuel for a fixed or portable wood stove. Depending on your resourcefulness, wood can range from free to thousands of dollars, based on your consumption and type of use.

Propane

Propane is a byproduct of the production of gasoline and the refining of crude oil. Propane has been used as a fuel since 1912, and it is the third most common fuel in the United States today, after gasoline and diesel. Most of the propane used in the United States is produced domestically.

Propane gas is an excellent fuel for running emergency generators. It is clean burning and readily available for delivery in many areas. Since propane gas is stored in a separate tank onsite, generators using it are usually not affected by the elements or by the types of mechanical disruptions that cause most residential power outages. For these reasons, manufacturers of emergency generators usually provide the option of using propane as a secondary fuel source. Propane generators are located outside the premises and are on standby mode until needed. When a homeowner is already using propane gas for heating or cooking, adding a propane-powered electric generator is always a good idea.

Either gasoline or diesel fuel, as shipped from the manufacturer, powers most portable generators. You may convert gasoline and diesel generators to propane, thereby providing the option of two sources of fuel. You will need to consult the manufacturer of your generator before attempting any conversion.

Batteries

Storage batteries are the essential component of any independent power system. They store energy, in addition to becoming a source of energy for use at a later time. They are extremely valuable when traditional (electric) or non-traditional (solar, wind, geothermal, etcetera) energy sources are not available. It's critical that you choose the right battery for the right application. These batteries could stand alone or form a battery bank that allows for longer output and the ability to support additional items that require electrical power. Here are some things to remember when considering batteries for use as an energy source in a SLAE situation:

- Battery storage has relatively high efficiency, as high as 90 percent or better. Be aware that the higher the efficiency, the higher the cost of the battery.

- Rechargeable batteries can be used as a rapid-response storage medium.

- Many off-the-grid domestic power systems rely on battery storage. Batteries designed for use in residential solar-electric systems are heavy-duty batteries designed to be discharged slowly and deeply. Typically, they range from two to twelve volts each, and a single battery can weigh up to several hundred pounds.

- There are basically three types of batteries recommended for alternative energy systems:

  ○ Flooded-type batteries are lead-acid batteries that can release hydrogen. Hydrogen is an extremely flammable gas, and as such the batteries must be vented if used inside.

  ○ Gel batteries are sealed, therefore there is no release of hydrogen.

  ○ Absorbed glass mat (AGM) batteries are leak proof and spill proof. In addition, they do no release hydrogen and are highly recommended for alternative energy systems.

The most popular batteries for energy storage and use include the following:

- Trojan T-105 Battery (flood type)

- ° These six-volt batteries are manufactured by Trojan Battery Company and are similar to golf-cart batteries. They weigh approximately sixty pounds, cost around $140, and will last for three to six years.
- L16H Battery (flood type)
  - ° These six-volt batteries are manufactured by a number of companies. They weigh about 120 pounds and cost around $350. Their life expectancy is six to eight years.
- Surrette Battery (flood type)
  - ° These batteries are made for larger and more demanding off-grid homes. They weigh more than 350 pounds and cost between $350 and $1,500 dollars. Surrette batteries last for twelve to fifteen years.
- HUP Solar One Battery (flood type)
  - ° These batteries are manufactured by General Battery. They are available in twelve- and twenty-four-volt capacities and are well suited for large solar arrays. A single HUP Solar One Battery can weigh from seven hundred to twenty-five hundred pounds. Their cost ranges from about three thousand dollars to twenty-five thousand dollars.

- Sun Xtender series by Concord Battery (AGM type)
  - ° These batteries contain an immobilized electrolyte, which means it can't be spilled. In addition, the series is maintenance free and an UL-recognized systems component. Their price ranges from $150 to more than $500.
- MK Gel Battery (Gel Type)
  - ° These batteries are maintenance free and good for renewable energy applications.

Petroleum

Petroleum is a term used to describe hydrocarbons, which primarily include oil and natural gas. Examples of refined (processed) hydrocarbons include gas, kerosene, and home-heating fuel. In everyday life, these resources are routinely available, but in a SLAE situation they become scarce and highly sought after. As such, your preps must include a predetermined amount of petroleum fuels, based on your needs. We store twenty gallons of kerosene (heater), sixty gallons of diesel (truck), thirty-five gallons of unleaded (generator and car), and ten gallons of white fuel (cooking or fuel lanterns). Below is more detail:

- Gasoline

- ° Gas is a volatile, flammable liquid made from petroleum and used as fuel in internal-combustion engines.
- ° For the Prepper, this will be the most common short-term fuel used. I say short-term because in a SLAE situation, there may come a time when gas is no longer available.
- ° You will need to store a sufficient quantity of gasoline to run any gas-powered cars, generators, or other applications.
- Diesel
  - ° Diesel is any fuel used in diesel engines.
  - ° Home-heating oil or fuel oil is nearly the same as diesel. Home-heating oil contains red dye to distinguish it from the diesel you buy at a gas station. The reason is that taxes are lower on home-heating fuel than on diesel fuel used for cars and trucks.
  - ° **Caution:** Although you can run home-heating fuel in your diesel engines, **do not do it**. If you get caught, there are severe penalties.
- Kerosene
  - ° Kerosene is a must for Preppers. Its applications include heaters, cooking stoves, and oil or kerosene lamps (e.g., Aladdin lamps).

- ° Kerosene is much safer to use than gasoline, natural gas, or propane. It can be purchased from your local fuel supplier, some gas stations, and hardware stores.
- ° I recommend storing enough kerosene to support your applications (heater, lamps, etcetera) for a minimum of three months.

Miscellaneous

In a SLAE situation you must always keep an open mind and be resourceful. There may come a time when you have to think outside of the box to find an alternative energy source. Examples of outside-of-the-box energy sources include the following:

- Alternator
  - ° Alternators can provide energy to charge batteries that can operate other twelve-volt items. It is easily adapted to any type of drive chain, including wind turbines, stationary bikes, and micro-hydropower.
- Coal
  - ° A great alternative to wood.
- Biomass briquettes
  - ° An alternative to wood or coal that involves the conversion of plant material (i.e., biomass) into

briquettes. For example, the biomass in garbage can be burned for heat or used as energy.

- Manure biofuel
  - ° Manure from pigs, chickens, and cows that can be burned for fuel once it has dried out.

Other Considerations

Medical Supplies

Although they are not specifically mentioned in the survival triangle, medical knowledge and medical supplies are critical to the Prepper. Obtaining medical knowledge could be as simple as taking a CPR or first-aid course, or arranging for access to a medically knowledgeable resource such as EMTs, nurses, physician assistants, or even doctors. Additional medical resources include books and guides that explain how to deal with specific circumstances in an emergency. In addition, it's important to have the proper basic medical supplies on hand. There may be many medical concerns during a SLAE situation, and you simply won't be able to cover them all, but being prepared for the basics will help. As a Prepper you will need to assemble an Emergency Bug-out Bag (EBOB). This is not to be confused with a Bug-out Bag (BOB), which contains personal items such as clothes, bug-out gear, and so on. An EBOB will contain emergency supplies and resources (e.g., books, printed material, pamphlets, etcetera) that will be useful should an emergency situation arise. An EBOB should also contain at least one to two months' supply of **any** medication you're taking. In a SLAE situation it's going to be extremely difficult to get refills or new prescriptions therefore the more you have on hand the better off you will be. For example, my son's an asthmatic and as such we have at least two months' supply of inhalers on hand at any one time. In addition we have access to the herb Mullein which can be used to help treat asthma. The EBOB must be easily accessible and ready to go at **all** times. Based upon your situation you may have multiple EBOBs; one for your shelter and one for your BOV. Your EBOB will contain some if not all of the medical items listed on the following pages.

Three categories of medical problems that may occur during a SLAE situation are immediately life threatening (ILT), serious, and minor. Some of these will arise due to contaminated water and poor living conditions. As discussed in the chapter titled, "Water," you must be able to properly filter and purify water. In addition, crowded living conditions can give rise to diseases such as tuberculosis, hepatitis A, or typhoid.

Immediately life-threatening conditions have the potential to cause immediate death unless medical attention is received. Examples include but are not limited to the following:

- ° Breathing
  - ▪ Airway, facial trauma, and/or burns
- ° Circulation
- ° Infection

Serious medical problems are debilitating or painful but typically don't cause death. Examples include but are not limited to the following:

- ° Broken bones
- ° Acute respiratory infection including upper respiratory infections such as
  - ▪ Bronchitis, colds, flu, pneumonia, and tuberculosis
- ° Tetanus
- ° Gangrene

Minor injuries or medical conditions are non-life threatening but should be addressed before they become more serious. Examples include but are not limited to the following:

- ° Allergies
- ° Digestive issues (e.g., diarrhea, vomiting)
- ° Sprains
- ° Cuts

Basic medical supplies should give you the capability to treat minor to serious issues. Given the vast array of medical possibilities, you're not going to be able to store everything. Store the essentials, which include but are no means limited to the following:

- Abdominal/pressure pad
- Ace bandages
- Adhesive bandages (assorted sizes and types)
- Alcohol (both 50 percent and 91 percent by volume)
- Alcohol wipes/antiseptic
- Antibiotic ointment (stock up on this)
- Betadine
- Burn Gel (a 2 percent lidocaine-based salve)
- Celox (stops bleeding in as little as thirty seconds)
- Gauze (assorted sizes and types)
- Hydrogen peroxide
- Ibuprofen/acetaminophen/Imodium/Benadryl/ Zyrtec or similar drugs
- Instant cold/hot Packs
- Iodine wipes and/or swabs
- Liquid Skin or similar substance
- NIOSH-certified N95 Mask (filters out H1N1)
- Splinter-removal kit
- Sting-relief wipes
- Super glue

- Tape, scissors, latex gloves, tweezers, and thermometer
- Tourniquet
- Wound-care kit with various sutures

Everyday Carry (EDC) Items

Everyday carry items are tools you keep with you at all times, regardless of where you go. These items could save your life or the lives of others at a moment's notice. EDC items are cleverly concealed, or in a few instances exposed, on your body. They may be worn around your neck. They may be on your belt or hidden inside the waistband of your pants. EDC items can be hidden around the liner of your baseball cap or under your shirt. They can be strapped to your leg or hidden under a long-sleeved shirt. There are many ways to conceal most items.

It's up to you to decide what items you will carry. Your EDC items will change, based on where you're going and what you're doing. For example, you would not carry the same EDC items on a business trip as you would on a hunting trip. While a knife or blade is extremely useful for field dressing a deer, the Transportation Security Administration (TSA) would never allow knives or any type of blade on an airliner. It's important to know your surroundings and what EDC items are useful and appropriate. Examples of EDC items that you may choose to carry include the following:

- Flashlight
  - ° Your EDC flashlight must be compact in size and bright enough to illuminate your target. For weight reasons it should use AA-size or preferably AAA-size batteries.
  - ° One good choice, the Streamlight Stylus Pro, is slightly larger than a pen and puts out forty-eight lumens of light.
- Leatherman or a similar multitool
- USB (flash drive)
  - ° Use this to store and gain access to data. In everyday life a USB drive is practical and sometimes necessary. In a SLAE, and assuming there is no power, a USB will not do you a whole lot of good.
- Pocket notebook
- Pen
  - ° Some manufacturers make pens that double as self-protection devices or flashlights.
- Folding knife
- Firearm
  - ° Be sure to follow state laws for carrying weapons.
- Paracord (a.k.a. parachute cord)

- ° This can be worn as a bracelet, but I don't recommend doing so because it calls attention to you, which is not good. I carry about thirty feet of paracord in my pocket.
- Lighter
  - ° Keep it simple and buy a disposable lighter.
- Thin wallet for carrying only the basics
- Piano wire
  - ° This can easily be hidden within the brim of your hat.
- Pepper spray
  - ° This useful item quickly disables any attacker.

Bug-out Vehicle (BOV)

How will you and your family get to your bug-out location (BOL)? For this you need a bug-out vehicle (BOV). In some instances families have multiple BOVs due to work locations, travel plans, and so on. My BOL is five hours away, so preparation is extremely important.

Here are several questions to ask when selecting a BOV:

- First and foremost, what can you afford?
  - ° Be reasonable here. Odds are you're not going to purchase that fifty-thousand-dollar top-of-the-line truck. When I purchased my truck,

I bought an older model that has reasonable mileage and works just fine. If I could not pay cash for a vehicle, then I would not buy it.

- What year of vehicle are you looking for?
  - ° Typically the older the car the lower the price but not always.
  - ° Cars made prior to 1984 have no computers or electronics that could be destroyed in an EMP (Electromagnetic Pulse).
- What type of engine are you looking for (i.e., gasoline, diesel, electric, or hybrid)?
- What types of fuel would you like your engine to use?
  - ° For example, diesel engines can burn multiple types of fuel, including home-heating fuel, biodiesel, and vegetable oil.
- Do you want or need four-wheel drive?
  - ° Four-wheel drive gives you the ability to go off-road, either in an emergency or to get to your BOL.
- How much fuel should your BOV be able to carry? Remember, not only do you need enough fuel to get to your BOL, you will need extra fuel due to its potential lack of availability in a SLAE situation. You must assume that gas stations will not have gas or diesel fuel readily available. This is for several reasons. The number-one reason is that

everyone will panic and quickly realize they need gas, because they're not prepared for the situation at hand. Lines will form, and tempers will flare. The second reason is that if the power goes out, the gas pumps will not work anyway. As mentioned previously, I personally observed this during 9/11. Consider the following:

- ° Is there room to install an external fuel tank?
- ° Is there room to carry extra gas cans?
- How much storage space do you need in your BOV?
  - ° Do you need the storage capacity of a truck, or will an SUV or smaller vehicle have enough space?
- How many passengers do you expect to carry?
- What body style do you want for your BOV? Consider these options:
  - ° A **truck** includes a cab for passengers (if desired) along with a cargo bed. It may be used to haul large, heavy loads and can have four-wheel drive.
  - ° Most **sport utility vehicles (SUVs)** have a higher carrying capacity than cars. They have up to three rows for passengers and can have four-wheel drive.

- ° A **sedan** typically has four doors, seating for five or six people, and a trunk for storage. Sedans come in many sizes.
- ° A **van** is a box-shaped vehicle that often has sliding side doors. Vans typically have higher clearance than cars (they sit higher off the ground).
- ° A **wagon** is a four-door vehicle with an open cargo area at the back and a rear lift-gate. Wagons can typically seat five or six people.
- ° A **crossover** is a combination of an SUV and a sedan, often without four-wheel drive.

My BOV is a Dodge truck 4X4 that runs on diesel. It has the quad cab. I wanted a truck for the cargo space. Though it is a short bed, I can carry an abundant amount of supplies, or I could put a camper shell on it and use it for shelter. I liked the diesel engine for its torque. We had a fifth wheel, and as we travelled through the mountains of the western United States we needed torque. The quad cab allows the family to drive in comfort and minimizes the kids fighting with one another. I have an in-bed sixty-nine-gallon diesel gas tank. In addition, I have a reinforced steel rack that I put in the receiver hitch on the truck, which allows me to carry an additional thirty to thirty-five gallons of diesel fuel. In total I can carry about 130 gallons of diesel. This gives me plenty of gas to get to my BOL and still have plenty left over. The 4X4 provides some comfort because I know that if I need to go off road to get to my BOL, I could. Finally, the diesel engine allows me to use alternative fuels and not have to rely on one type (like a gasoline engine). I can burn home-heating oil, vegetable oil, biodiesel, and with a lubricating agent, some kerosene. In a SLAE situation I want the flexibility to know I can use multiple fuels due to the fact that diesel may not be available.

It's critical to have spare parts for your BOV and to know how to remove and install them. Essential spare parts may include starters, alternators, fuel pumps, filters, hoses, oil, and brakes. Once again, the idea is to be prepared before you have to be prepared.

Bug-out Directions (BODs)

The next thing to consider is how you will navigate to your BOL. It may sound easy enough to grab your GPS and head to the nearest major highway—but that would be a mistake. In a SLAE situation, major highways will be crowded with people all trying to do the same thing: get out of town. These major highways will be the only route that the majority of people know. When cars run out of gas, the highways will become death traps. People will panic, and even more cars will block the highways.

Now you probably see the need to plan your escape route. You should have at least two escape routes that use back roads. First, plan a route that uses secondary roads and avoids major highways. Second, create an additional route that uses tertiary roads. You may be traveling the back roads of America, but the outcome will be to arrive safely at your BOL. You can simply handwrite each route, or you can highlight a map. Either way, the goal is to provide clear, easy-to-read directions to your BOL.

You must assume that your GPS will not work. This could be the case for several reasons. First of all, satellites may be unavailable or shut down. Second, solar flares, which induce geomagnetic storms, travel at the speed of light and affect GPS receivers, typically beginning one hour after eruption. Third, coronal mass ejections, which induce geomagnetic storms and reach the earth one to three days after eruption, have the threat level of solar events. And finally, there is jamming, which is an intentional act by a person, entity, or country to block and confuse the GPS receiver. GPS receivers are extremely sensitive and therefore easy to jam.

If your bug-out location is within the United States, your bug-out directions should include an atlas and maps of any counties or states you plan to travel through. I suggest you photocopy your bug-out route and then laminate it for protection. You should create copies of your BODs and place them in each BOV. In addition, I highly recommend that you identify your escape routes by using highlighters on the map itself. Use a different color to mark each route. At night and during times of stress, the highlighted portion of the map will provide contrast relative to the background of the map. The goal is to make it easy to see and easy to navigate. Once again, make copies of the highlighted map, laminate them, and place a copy in each BOV.

I highly encourage you to drive each of your emergency routes to get a better sense of what you might encounter while bugging out. While driving each route, observe your surroundings and mark the following on your map or BODs:

- Major landmarks
- Sources of water
- Safe places to rest if you need them
- The time it takes to get to your BOL
- The number of vehicles you pass on your way (You don't want your route to be too crowded with people or cars)
- Grocery stores and gas stations
- Local law-enforcement offices
- The types of roads you're driving on (e.g., two-lane or country roads)

Finally, make sure there are no major obstacles on your escape route that would prohibit you from reaching your BOL. For example, let's assume that you need to get to the Upper Peninsula of Michigan from elsewhere in the state. You should not create a route that includes traveling over the Mackinac Bridge because the bridge could be damaged or closed to traffic. Why take that chance? Although an alternative route may increase your driving time to the Upper Peninsula, you can be assured that you will arrive at your destination without problems.

Communication and Media

Your primary shelter and BOL should have multiple forms of communication means. These will keep you informed of the current conditions and well as future plans. For this section I assume that cell phones, land lines, internet, and computers are unable to provide any form of communication for various reasons. When we think of communication, TV immediately comes to mind. However, in a SLAE scenario the odds are high that there will be no power. Even if there is power, there's no guarantee that a TV signal will be available. You will need to rely on other, less formal, means of communication. Below are examples of some useful communication devices and their characteristics:

- Shortwave radios
  - ○ Shortwave radios can receive radio transmissions on frequencies between three and thirty MHz, which enables worldwide communications and the ability to stay informed. In addition, shortwave radios can be heard from thousands of miles away and are extremely economical to purchase.
- MURS (Multi-Use Radio Service)
  - ○ MURS are two-way radios with a limited transmitter-power output of two watts. The radios are capable of transmitting three to four miles based on line-of-sight, and one to two miles with minimal blockage from buildings or trees. MURS are economical to purchase and practical, as they transmit and receive on frequencies relatively unknown to the general population.
- CB radios (Citizen Band radios)
  - ○ CB radios can transmit no farther than 155 miles per FCC regulations, but in practice, they transmit no more than four to twenty miles based on line-of-sight. They are economical to purchase and would be a great addition to any Prepper's stores.
- GMRS (General Mobile Radio Service)

- ○ GMRS radios require a valid GMRS license to operate. They are FM/UHF radios that operate at short distances only. They are moderately priced.
- Ham radio (amateur radio)
  - ○ Ham radios require a license and transmit on frequency modulation (FM) and single sideband (SSB). Ham radios receive and transmit across cities, regions, countries, or continents and are moderately to high priced. Ham radios are still highly recommended for the Prepper.

Lighting

The focus of this section will be portable lighting. Portable lighting is used whenever your primary light sources are not available, regardless of reason. For example, in a rainstorm the power goes out, and you need light. One would typically light an oil lamp or bring out the flashlights. These are examples of portable lighting in that they are easily accessible and lightweight. Furthermore, they produce sufficient lumens (a measure of the total "amount" of visible light emitted by a source), and they can travel with you wherever you may require it. In addition to preparing for portable lighting, make sure you store the proper energy source, as your lighting will require a power source such as a generator, a battery bank (as discussed in the chapter titled "Energy"), batteries (sized AAA, AA, C, D, etcetera), lamp oil, kerosene, and so on. Below are examples of lighting options and their characteristics. This list is by no means exhaustive, and these are only examples:

- Flashlights, headlamps, lanterns, and fluorescent strips
  - ° The majority use standard batteries. The cost is relatively inexpensive, dependent on brand, and they can provide redundant lighting sources for family members (i.e., more than one light source). These types of lights vary in lumens and weight for portability.
  - ° Standardize on one type of battery for **all** your flashlights. For example, I highly recommend AAA-size batteries as they can be used in flashlights and headlamps.
- Solar lights
  - ° Solar lights are recharged by the sun via a solar panel. They have several advantages, such as using a renewable energy source (i.e., the sun) and can be easily found at any local hardware store. In addition to being portable they are inexpensive, ranging from four dollars to sixty dollars.

- Light sticks
  - ° Light sticks are easy to store and use. They have a short life span of one to sixteen hours.
  - ° If you chose to purchase light sticks, I recommend buying in small bulk units on eBay or other sources. I prefer the yellow-colored light sticks.
- Candles
  - ° I highly recommend honey candles over wax perfumed candles. Candles are portable but do present a fire hazard due to the open flame.
- Dynamo flashlights/lanterns
  - ° Dynamo flashlight/lanterns use the Faraday principle of electromagnetic energy to eliminate the need for batteries. Basically, by cranking a handle, energy is created and then stored in rechargeable battery cells. This stored energy is used to power the bulb. As the flashlight is used it has to be recharged (cranked) to provide sufficient lighting.
- Kerosene lamps
  - ° Kerosene lamps come in many forms, including Aladdin Lamps, and as stated use kerosene as a fuel source. The amount of light required is adjusted by a wick. They are easily transported

from location to location but do present a fire hazard.

- White-fuel lanterns
  - ◦ White-fuel lanterns are available from many manufacturers, with the most recognizable being Coleman. The fuel is easily purchased at local retailers, and I would highly recommend buying extra mantels, glass globes, and pumps. White-fuel lanterns are portable and reasonably priced, but they are a fire hazard if used inappropriately.
- LEDs (Light Emitting Diodes)
  - ◦ LEDs come in various types, from fixed lighting to lanterns to those worn on your head or body. LEDs can operate on everything from twelve-volt battery banks to AAA-size batteries. Most portable LEDs worn on the head or body operate off of AAA-size or AA-size batteries.
- Propane lanterns
  - ◦ Typical propane lanterns use one-pound propane cylinders, which are sold at local retailers (e.g., Target, Walmart, etcetera). They are easy to use, convenient, portable, and cost effective. Once again they pose a fire hazard if used inappropriately.

- Oil lamps
  - Oil lamps operate off of lamp oil (i.e., liquid petroleum). The amount of light desired is adjusted by raising the wick up or down. Oil lamps are both portable and cost-effective. They pose a fire hazard if used inappropriately.

Couponing

You may wonder why couponing is included in this book. The reason is simple: Most people who decide to prep become overwhelmed at the cost. The first thing to remember is that you don't have to buy everything at once. As previously mentioned, Prepping is an ongoing adventure that will last your lifetime. If you're like me, you will constantly find items to add to your stores, and they don't have to be expensive or name brand.

In the following pages I describe ways to use coupons to increase your stores. I focus on food and household goods, as those offer the biggest bang for the buck in the couponing world. First of all, you and your family need to determine your level of brand loyalty. Do you buy only one brand of soup or cereal, or are you open to other brands (including generics)? The more flexible you are, the more choices you will have. Keep in mind that brand-name items typically cost more, and they are not always on sale when compared to store and generic brands. In addition, I've found that certain name-brand coupons are almost impossible to find and rarely if at all on sale. From here on, I'll assume you're open to different brands, you've purchased and tried several store and generic labels, and you liked them. Now, it's time to find some coupons.

The first place to start is the Sunday newspaper. There you'll find three sources of coupon books: Red Plum, Proctor & Gamble (P&G), and Smart Source. These coupon books are not in the Sunday paper every week. A great website that tells which coupon books will be in your Sunday paper is www.sunday-couponpreview.com. This site offers a service that will send you an email, about midweek, describing which coupon books will be available that Sunday.

Many coupons are also available online. Websites to check include the following:

- Coupons.com
- Smartsource.com
- Redplum.com

You can also download coupons directly from vendor websites. You typically have to sign up with an email address and agree to occasionally receive marketing information.

There are also websites that sell coupons in bulk. You simply select the coupons you need and pay a small fee. The fee is based on the number of coupons, the value of the coupon savings, small administrative charges, and shipping costs. This may sound like a lot of money, but it really isn't. For example, let's say you want to buy ten Old Spice deodorant coupons that are for one dollar off the product. The fee might be calculated as follows:

10 coupons X $.10 (10 percent of the $1.00 coupon face value) + $.50 (administrative fee) + $.75 (shipping fee) = $2.25

The administrative fee is charged only once per order, so if you purchased other coupons along with your Old Spice deodorant coupons the administrative fee for your order would still be just fifty cents. Two examples of these coupon-clipping services are Couponclippers.com and Thecouponmaster.com.

It's important to shop at grocery stores that double your coupons. Doubling of your coupons simply means that if you use a fifty-cent coupon the store will double its value, making it worth one dollar. I've never seen a grocery store double coupons beyond a one-dollar coupon value. When we first started couponing there were no grocery stores in our area that doubled coupons, so we had to travel forty-five minutes to reach one. The gas almost cost more than the savings, but the trip still made financial sense.

We soon learned that some of the best deals could be found at stores other than grocery stores. Drugstores like Walgreens and CVS had stellar deals for our needs. These stores run great sales on necessities like toothpaste, deodorant, feminine products, school supplies, first-aid supplies, cereal, and other household items. We purchase items when they're on sale and when reward cash or similar incentives are offered. Reward cash is basically a coupon that the store gives out for use at a later time. For example, suppose that Crest toothpaste is on sale for two dollars with one dollar in reward cash. We buy the toothpaste for two dollars, use a one-dollar coupon, and receive one dollar in reward cash. This essentially makes the toothpaste free! The math looks like this:

$2.00 Crest – $1.00 coupon – $1.00 reward cash = $1.00 due at time of purchase, with a $1.00 reward cash to use at the next visit

Many stores have BOGO (buy one get one) sales. Sometimes the item is BOGOF (buy one get one free), and sometimes it's BOGO half off. When you purchase two items as part of a BOGO sale, most stores still allow you to use two manufacturer coupons (one per item)—and you can use your reward cash, too!

Keep in mind that each store has separate policies on couponing, and the easiest way to learn them is to ask for the store policy. Stores may also offer some type of customer-loyalty discount card. I recommend signing up for these, as you can use them to save money on food and in some cases fuel. Stores such as Kroger allow you to load coupons on the card directly from their website and then redeem them at checkout. This beats having to carry around two hundred paper coupons.

In couponing you have to be patient. The item you need or want will not always be on sale, nor will there always be a coupon for that item. Coupons are seasonal, meaning that the coupons you find in October will not be the same as those you find in November. Most coupons do expire, so keep track of their dates—but don't feel like you have to use every one. Don't buy an item with a coupon if it's not something you want or need.

Remember the following: Buy what you eat and eat what you buy.

Staying organized is the tough part. With hundreds of coupons, where do you put them all? We chose a simple system that uses index cards and plastic note-card holders. We purchased five of these holders and labeled them "Hygiene," "Dairy," "Groceries," "First Aid," and "Household." We then labeled the index cards by the brand and category of the item. For example, coupons for Crest toothpaste go in the

"Hygiene" index-card box behind the card labeled "Crest." I like things to be quick and easy, so this works for me. There are more formal systems out there. Some people use binders, while others use shoeboxes. Your goal is to find a system that works for you.

Couponing was the tool that allowed us to begin Prepping. It allowed us to purchase not only food but also first-aid and household items to put in our Prepping storage at a reduced or reasonable price. We still use coupons today, but we only buy what we'll use. We are not the type of people who purchase two hundred of one item simply because we have coupons and we can. In addition, my wife and I freely share our couponing knowledge to those who are interested. As the third tenant of Prepping discusses, you need to reach out and help others when you can, before they reach out to you.

What Do We Do If There Is a SLAE Situation?

If a SLAE situation occurs, there will be a timeframe where you shelter in place, dependent on the magnitude and effects of the event. Sheltering in place simply means staying where you are, typically in your primary shelter or house, if the circumstances allow. This is why you need to be prepared. Opinions vary across the board on this timeframe, but it could range from one day to two weeks. The timeframe will vary based on the type of SLAE scenario, your provisions, the severity of the situation, your comfort level, the availability of a BOV/BOL, time of the year, and so on. This timeframe (i.e., one day to two weeks) allows for the emotions of the event to be processed and hopefully better understood.

During the initial stage of any SLAE situation there will be confusion, lack of direction, chaos, and many unanswered questions. The population will be looking for guidance on what steps to take next, as well as information about the situation (i.e., what caused it, how long it will continue, when the electricity will be on, where to find first-aid stations, how to get food, etcetera). All levels of government—local, county, state, and federal—will be extremely selective about when, how, and what they communicate. When you shelter in place, you do not expose yourself or your loved ones to the chaos (i.e., to other people who are not prepared).

Within weeks after a SLAE situation, the landscape will change dramatically. Individuals and families who aren't properly prepared will begin to panic. They will begin to realize that if assistance hasn't arrived, it most likely isn't going to arrive. Their limited food and supplies will have been consumed, and the grocery stores and hardware stores will have nothing else available. Most people's biggest concern will be the lack of food and water. These individuals will begin to look outside their usual sources and to ask others for basic supplies. Maybe others will give, but maybe they won't. As time goes by, people will become desperate. In order to protect their loved ones and save their lives, they may do things they would never have done previously. When this stage arrives, and preferably some time before, head to your bug-out location. If you have no BOL or are unable to reach it, you will need to secure your shelter as best you can. You will secure your shelter based on materials, resources, and knowledge. In addition, you should consider the time of year, size of the shelter, location of the shelter, distance from a large population, and terrain surrounding your shelter.

If you're able to bug out, you will need to make sure your bug-out directions are ready, and all the supplies you plan to take are sorted and organized. You want to minimize the chaos of leaving and make sure your bug-out vehicle is ready. It's important that you bug out at night. It would be too obvious if you did it during the day, and you may attract unwanted attention. You should also arrive at your BOL in the night if at all possible. If that's not possible, you need to minimize your daytime driving.

In both your primary shelter and your BOL, you need to be constantly aware of the noise you produce as well as the light you use at night. There will be people out there searching for any sign of generators, guns, cars, or machinery that would signal the possible presence of food, fuel, shelter, or even ammunition. Walking around outdoors with flashlights allows others to identify your position and therefore compromises your location. Indoor lighting does the same but also lets people know that you may have some form of electricity. One recommendation is to make blackout curtains or shades for the windows for your primary shelter or BOL.

You must also be careful with your communications. Sixty-foot antennas can be seen from a distance and let others know your location. It's best to use antennas that are strung from tree to tree, or at lower levels. Keep in mind that people will be monitoring the airwaves for any type of communication. They will then determine if it's short-range or long-range communication. If they find short-range communication, they can easily zero in on your location. Transmit as little as possible. You do not want to reveal your location.

This shelter, either where you shelter in place or bug out to, will now provide you and your family the necessities of life, but it won't remove the challenges that remain ahead. How well you prepared will determine the actions you take or may have to take. Whether it be hunting, fishing, trapping, gardening, working with community, bartering, or even doing nothing, you will still have to continue your Christian Prepper lifestyle. How you take these actions, and how successful you will be, is dependent upon the experience and resourcefulness of your family or group. The ironic thing is there could be a SLAE within a SLAE, and in both cases you have to be prepared.

In conclusion, I would state that we're all aware that there is no guarantee in life, let alone in the decisions we make. But what I do know is that Prepping can negate a negative outcome in many SLAE situations but not all. Throughout the Bible, Jesus warns man of past and future Significant Life Altering Events and gives guidance on how to prepare. Although being physically prepared is not the same as having faith, I believe the two go hand-in-hand. Having faith allows us to be prepared while being prepared allows us to focus on our faith. I hope you found the information in this handbook useful as well as enjoyable. My sole purpose was to provide exposure to the Christian Prepper, the Christian Prepper lifestyle, and the options that Christian Preppers may consider. The questions you now have to answer are what outcome do you hope for, and are you ready to become a Prepper?

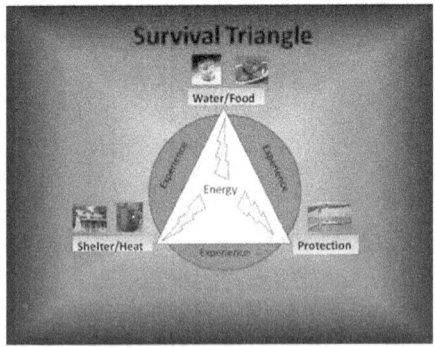

Key to Acronyms

BO: Bug Out

BOB: Bug-out Bag

BODs: Bug-out Directions

BOGO: Buy One Get One (typically 50 percent off or free)

BOL: Bug-out Location

BOV: Bug-out Vehicle

EBOB: Emergency Bug-out Bag (contains only medical supplies)

EDC: Everyday Carry

GOOD: Get out of Dodge; same as BO

ILT: Immediately Life Threatening

MRE: Meal-Ready-to-Eat

NVGs: Night-vision Goggles

SLAE: Significant Life Altering Event

TEOTWAWKI: The End of the World As We Know It

WROL: World without Rule or Law

Bibliography

Army, U. (n.d.). *Emergency Drinking Water Disinfection Procedure.* Retrieved October 6, 2011, from Emergency Drinking Water Disinfection Procedure: phc.amedd.army.mil/PHC%20Resource%20Library/31-008-1004.pdf

FEMA. (2004, August). *Food and Water in an Emergency.* Retrieved October 6, 2011, from www.fema.gov: http://www.fema.gov/txt/library/f&web.txt

Harison, E. L. (2006). *General Freezing Information.* Retrieved October 6, 2011, from National Center for Home Food Preservation: http://www.uga.edu/nchfp/how/freeze/containers.html

Health, N. I. (n.d.). *Dehydration.* Retrieved October 6, 11, from MedlinePlus: http://www.nlm.nih.gov/medlineplus/ency/article/000982.htm

Health, W. S. (2011, November 20). *Public Health and Response.* Retrieved October 6, 2011, from Purifying Household Water: http://www.doh.wa.gov/phepr/handbook/purify.htm

Hunt, H. (2008, April 4). *What Exactly Does the Term "Homesteading" Mean?* Retrieved October 6, 2011, from Mother Earth News: http://www.motherearthnews.com/ask-our-experts/what-does-homesteading-mean.aspx

InvestmentWatch. (2011, October 25). *WARNING: There are four million preppers in the United States today are preparing for a mega-disaster.* Retrieved November 6, 2011, November, from InvestmentWatch: http://investmentwatchblog.com/warning-there-are-four-million-preppers-in-the-united-states-today-are-preparing-for-a-mega-disaster/

Bibliography

Nations, F. a. (2011, July 22). *Wood Energy.* Retrieved October 6, 2011, from Food and Agriculture Organization of the United Nations: http://www.fao.org/forestry/energy/en/

Prevention, C. f. (2006, May 27). *Center for Disease Control and Prevention.* Retrieved October 6, 2011, from Water Treatment Methods: http://wwwnc.cdc.gov/travel/page/water-treatment.htm

Riverwalker. (2009). *Mission Statement.* Retrieved 10 22, 2011, from Prepper.org: http://prepper.org/

Unknown. (n.d.). *MURS Two Way Radio and Security Equipment.* Retrieved October 6, 2011, from murs-radio.com: http://shop.murs-radio.com/MURS-Alert-Transmitter-MAT.htm

Unknown, A. (2011, June 20). *The Water In You.* Retrieved October 6, 2011, from USGS: http://ga.water.usgs.gov/edu/propertyyou.html

www.ingramcontent.com/pod-product-compliance
Lightning Source LLC
Chambersburg PA
CBHW070155290526
45789CB00002B/784